duchess
of Northumberland

duchess
of Northumberland

LITTLE BOOK OF

JAMS, JELLIES
AND PRESERVES

The
History
Press

Front cover image: © iStockphoto
Internal illustrations: © Oliver Goodson

First published 2013

The History Press
The Mill, Brimscombe Port
Stroud, Gloucestershire, GL5 2QG
www.thehistorypress.co.uk

British Library Cataloguing in Publication Data.
A catalogue record for this book is available from the British Library.

ISBN 978 0 7524 9450 0

Typesetting and origination by The History Press
Printed in Great Britain

INTRODUCTION

BY THE DUCHESS OF NORTHUMBERLAND

I'm really pleased to be able to share with you some of the treasures from the archive here at Alnwick and to think that these wonderful old recipes will now be seen and enjoyed again, and cooked too, I hope!

There are some wonderful things here based on native British hedgerow fruit, herbs and spices that are charmingly described in their original language that is surprisingly easy to understand. Who could not want to make 'a blanc manger for one that is sicke' or be tempted to add 'Sinamond' to

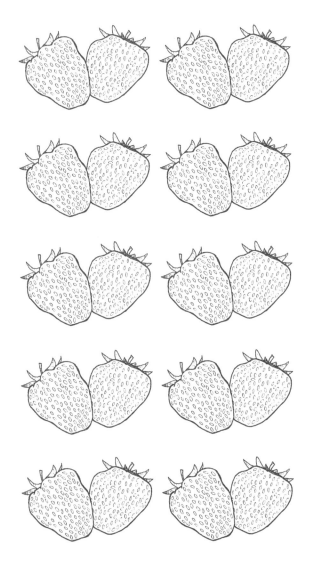

a recipe for fruit that is 'thorowe ripe'? I'm also tempted by a 'Sirupe of Rindes of Orenges or Lemons' since it promises that it 'strengtheneth the stomache, the braine and the hearte' – what more could anyone ask for?

Most of all, though, I think it's wonderful that we are able to include what is thought to be the oldest recipe for marmalade made in this country from Edith Beale's recipe book of 1576 and still stored in the archive at the castle. Edith Beale was the great-great-great-great grandmother of the first Duchess of Northumberland and her recipe book has passed from grandmother to grand-daughter down the ages – it's good to think that link is being continued.

We've recently been able to get the marmalade manufactured again by Mercers Jams and it's very exciting that this year it will be available in shops throughout the country in versions using both oranges and quinces. The quince pre-dates the introduction of oranges to this country and is a wonderful fruit that has the additional charm of having aphrodisiac properties!

Reading through the book it is both an inspiration and a kind of 'intravenous' history lesson that brings the whole world of still rooms and household management to life and allows us to see how aspects of it are still very relevant to how we live now.

I hope you enjoy this compilation of some of the very best recipes from the archive as much as we've enjoyed putting it together.

Her Grace The Duchess of Northumberland

TO PRESERVE
CITRONS

*T*ake three Citrons and pare them cleane
and quarter them then pike out the coare
then laye them in water two dayes and two nightes
but you must not change them. So done take a
pottell of white wine and set it a Boylinge in a
brasen panne. When it dothe boile take three
whites of egges and then cleare the white wine
with an egge at once and skimme upp the skome
as it riseth. When it is verie cleare then put in the
Citrons and let them boyle. You must set a skillet

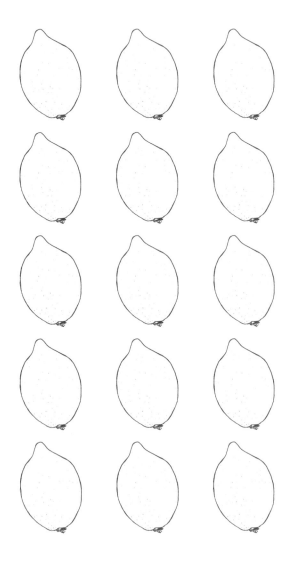

of faire water by the fire and let it boile and so putt it upp 4 times as it boileth. When you can put a rushe thorough the Citron then take upp the Citrons and laye them in a faire linnen clothe upon a bourde and so let it all night. You must warme the clothe. This is the boilinge of the Citrons. Then make the sirupe with a pint of rose water and a quarte of faire water and two pounde of white suger. Set it a boilinge when it dothe boile take 3 whites of egges and cleare the sirupe with one white at once and skimme upp the skimme as it riseth. So done put in the Citrons and let it boyle till it be cleare when they be colde take them upp and put them in a gallye potte.

TO PRESERVE
ORENGES

*T*ake xx orenges of the smothest that you can gett and pare them as thinne as you can. Then cut them in the midest and pike out the kernells cleane. Then laye them in faire water and you must change them two times a daye. They must bye in water three dayes. Then take a gallon of old white wyne and set it a boyling in a brasen panne. So done take the whites of eight eggs and cleare it withall. Skimme upp the skimme as it risethe. it must be verie cleare. If it

be not cleare straine it with a faire linnen clothe.
Then put in the orenges. You must tourne them
still and let them boile. When you can put a
rushe thorough the orenges then take them upp
and laye them one by one uppon a faire bourde
all night. So done take a quarte of rose water and
a quarte of faire water and 8 pounds of the whitest
suger that you can gett and set it a boylinge in a
brasen panne. So done take the whites of 8 egges
and cleare it withall and it must be so cleare that
you maie see a heare at the bottome if it be not
cleare inough you maie straine it. Then putt in
the orenges but see there be no blackes in them
and let them boile. Turne them still and take
heade that they seethe not to longe. if they doe
they will look blacke. Take them upp when they
looke cleare and let the sirrupe boyle. Then putt
them in a gallye potte and put a fewe Cloves at
the bottome of the potte.

TO MAKE CONSERVES
OF BARBARIES

*T*ake your Barberies and pike them and boile them in Claret wine till they be broken then straine them and put to everie pounde of Barbaries one pounde of suger then boile them againe till they be something thicke. Then put them into a vessell of glasse or into a gallie potte and strewe suger somwhat thicke uppon the Conserve. When it is whotte suger will preserve it. Your Barbaries must be wayed when they be piked.

TO MAKE CONSERVES
OF ROSES OR ANYE
OTHER KINDE
OF FLOWERS

*T*ake the red buddes of roses and plucke them and Cut of the white of the leaves and take to a pounde of rose leaves one pounde of suger finelye beaten. Then beate your rose leaves in a morter and beate them verie small and as you beate them put a quarter of a pounde of suger therin.

Then take it upp and put it into a broade mouthed glasse and stoppe your glasse verie well for taking aire and set it in the sonne. And so use it for the space of 4 dayes taking it out of the glasse and put it into a morter and beate it puttinge to it a quarter of a pounde of suger and beate it till you can perceave no parte of the suger and at the iiij dayes ende put it in the foresaid glasse being stopped verie close you must set it in the sonne the space of xv or xx daies and keepe it and so you must doe to all others.

FOR THE PRESERVINGE OF DAMSONES IN SIRUPE

*T*ake 3 poundes of damsons and 2 poundes of suger verie finelie beaten. Then take an earthen panne and put therin rosewater and a litle suger and put onto the bottome of the panne and set the damsones one by one as maie lye in the same panne. Then cast a good quantitie of suger uppon them. This done set it uppon the imbers boilinge verie softlye keping them from breakinge. And being well boiled take them and put them into the vessell that you minde to keepe them in and stoppe them verie close. So kepinge them for a fortnight or 3 weekes. Then boile it againe putting in also more suger to them till your sirupe be verie thicke. This done put them againe into the preservative vessell putting therto whole cloves and Sinamon Cut in peces and cast uppon the suger somwhat thick and stoppe them not before they are through Colde. It is best to put the same vessell in sande in Somer time. And as you are declared to Order these damsones so you maie preserve cheryes.

FOR THE
PRESERVINGE
OF PEACHES

*T*ake peaches being thorowe ripe and pare
    them verye thine you maye if you list cut
out the stones in the sides. Then take to everye
pint of faire water a pounde of suger being well
beaten and put as muche water as will Cover your
peaches and somwhat more. Then set the water
and suger over the fire and put therto ii or iii
whites of egges and so let it boile untill the whites

of the egges be harde. Then straine it. And after it is so boyled skome the panne verie Cleane. This done put in your sirupe and the peaches so let them boyle together untill the sirupe be verie thicke. Then use them as before you used the damsons. If they be white peaches put Cloves to them. If red put Cloves and Sinamon.

TO PRESERVE QUINCES

*U*se them as before you used your peaches save you must put into your water at the first boilinge therof a fewe of the paringes and the Cores of your quinces and let it so boile together a quarter of an hower. Then use it as you did your peaches save only you must seethe them but once untill your sirupe be as thicke as a gellye.

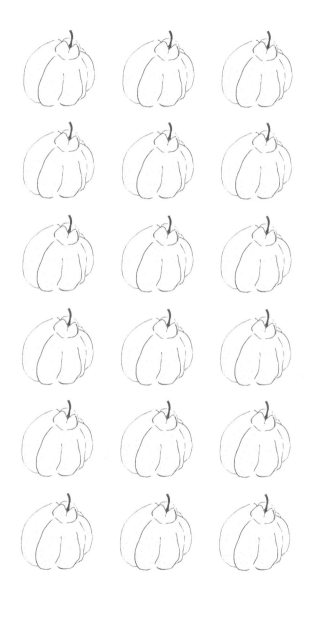

ANOTHER WAYE

Take the quinces and pare them and core them and take wardens and pare them and Cut them in half. Then take an earthen potte and put therin your quinces and wardens But you must put your wardens in the bottome and at the toppe Castinge amongest them suger Sinamon unbeaten and whole Cloves. If the same potte be a pottell then put therto a quarte of muskadell or pleasant Claret wine of a good Colour. Then stoppe the same with past and set him into an oven as whote as you make it for the bakinge of manchets and let him stande for the space of a daye and a night in the oven. Then take him out of the oven but you must not open the same ii or iij dayes after. Then put them into a vessel that you list to keepe them in but keepe them Close.

TO PRESERVE
BARBARIES

*T*ake some of the worse of the Barbaries
and seeth them in water and when they
have well sodden straine the water and put as
muche suger to it as will make your Sirupe
thicke. Then let the same seethe and when it hath
sodden a litle while let it stande till it be almost
Colde, and then put in your Barbaries. This done
put in your Barbaries and let them boile in the
same liquor softlye untill the sirupe be thicke.
Then take a litle warme rosewater and if ye see

them shrincke to muche take them upp and let the sirupe boile till it be thicke. Then take it of and put therto Sinamon unbrused and whole cloves and when it is Almost Colde put the Barbaries therto.

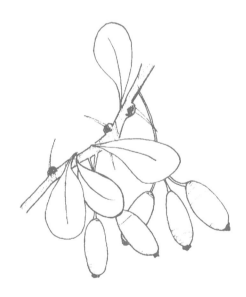

TO PRESERVE
BROME FLOWERS

Gather the buddes when they be half blowen and water them in water untill the bitternes be gone. Then put them into your sirupe of orenges when It is half boiled and boile them a litle.

TO PRESERVE
WALNUTTES

Take walnuttes before the shell be harde and laye them in Cleane water untill the bitternes be gone. Then take to everye pint of Cleare water one pound of suger and take whites of egges and stirre the water and that together. Then set it over the fire and let it seethe untill the whites of egges are harde. Then straine it as before and your panne being verie cleane skoured seethe it againe and therewith put your walnuttes until it be thicke like sirupe.

Then keepe it close for a fortnight or iij wekes
and then seethe it againe and when it hath boiled
a litle while put therto some rosewater warmed
and so do to orenges

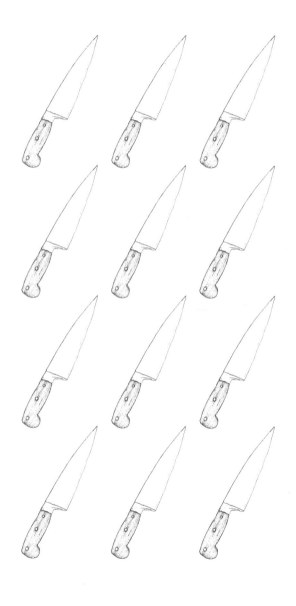

TO MAKE
QUODINYAKE

*T*ake quinces pare then and Cut everie
quince in iiij peces and core them
putting to everie pounde of quinces ij pounds of
suger and set them on the fire and beinge readie
to seethe them with whites of egges. And when
it shall beginne to waxe red prove with a knife.
And if it will Cut then straine it into your boxe
with a fine strainer.

TO MAKE MARMALADE OF QUINCES

First seethe the quinces unpared and uncoared in faire water untill they be somthinge softe. Then take them and pare them and Cut of all the best from the Coare. Then stampe them in a faire morter or in some faire vessell and so straine them. That done take to everye pounde of quinces 3 quarters of a pounde of suger. You must put your suger being finelye beaten into an earthen potte and let it stande upon the fire till it seethe. Then take it of and straine it and then put it into the quinces and stirre them all the while they doe seethe and beinge half sodden put therto a litle rosewater and when it will Cut with a knife put it into your boxe. To vj pounds of quinces you must take iiij pounds and an half of suger But to this proportion you must not exceede iiij pintes of faire water and so further to take of water as your proportion of the other stuffe is.

TO POWDER BROME FLOWERS

Gather the buddes thereof if you can as manye as will fill your potte in a daye it is best and first laye a line of white salt in the bottome of your potte and then a line of the same flowers and a line of white salt. Fill your vessell therwith as full as you can thrust them downe and let them so stande a daye. And if they shall shrincke fill them upp with flowers. Afterwarde fill it upp with vergis and laye a good deale of salt uppon it and stoppe it Close.

TO KEEPE BARBARIES
TO DRESSE MEATE

*T*ake the worse of them and seethe them in faire water and straine them and when the liquor is colde put it to your Barbaries cleane piked and so stoppe them. And if the moulde mutche all to washe them with that liquor and boile that liquor againe and skime it and when it is colde put in your Barbaries.

TO MAKE CLEARE
MARMALADE
OF QUINCES

*F*irst take the quinces and wipe them verie cleane with a faire clothe: then cutte them in quarters and cut the coare verie clearlye out of them. If the quinces be greate then cutte them in half quarters or lesse and then put them in a newe earthen potte which hath bene occupied with no other thinge but onlye with quinces fillinge the same potte with the Cutt quinces upp to the verye

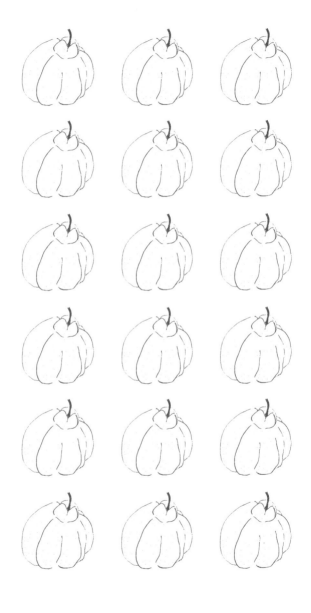

brimme. And to a pottell of quinces ye must put a wine pint of Cleare water: and then cover the potte Close with an earthen potlidde and make a softe fire of Coales without anye smoke round about the potte so that it touche not the potte for burninge of them. Shake the potte betwene your hands so as the quinces beinge nethermost maie come to the toppe. But in anywise beware you breake not the quinces in shakinge of them for then it will never be cleare. And when they be verie tender take them from the fire and let them stande Close covered till they be but luke warme. Then take a pece of newe clothe which you will occupie to no other purpose. Canvas is best when it is shrunke in faire water and dryed againe: and then put your quinces into it that your cleare sirupe maie runne through the clothe into a faire bason or some other thinge that you maye see it be cleare. And when it will runne no more of it self through then wringe them so long as ye can gette anye cleare sirupe out and no longer. Beate your suger verie small and looke the same be verie white and of the best ye can gette.

Then put your suger and sirupe together into a faire skillet beinge the more handsome to take from the fire and so set the same on. Your fire must be quicke and cleare without smoke and ye must stirre it well with a cleane spoone. And when it hath sodden a while that the skome dothe arise take it from the fire and skemme it and set it on again iij or iiij time at the least. And when it is sodden inough it will rise upp to the toppe of the skillet. Then set it from the fire: if it stande at a staye and fall not streight then put it out in time into suche thinges as you will keepe it and let it stande till it be colde. Then will it be good jellye: if it be to muche sodden it wilbe as harde as glewe. And as for the quantitie of suger you maie doe as you list. A pounde of suger to a pint of sirupe wilbe well that it maie keepe longe: If it take suger or seething it wilbe moulded.

TO MAKE
MARMALADE

*T*ake suger ij pounds and a half to iij pounds of quinces a quarte of water put the one half into the suger and in thother half you must putt the whites of 3 egges and beate the water and them together. Then seethe your quinces in water and when they be well sodden you must straine them through a pece of Canvas but keepe half the water into your suger as it clarifie the And when your suger is well clarified you must put your quinces after you have strained them into it and so let them boile always stirringe it untill it be boyled inoughe.

TO PRESERVE
ORENGES

ake of the thickest rynded orenges and pare of the Uppermost rinde verie thinne: then cut them longe wayes: pick out the kernells and laie them in water ij or iij dayes shiskinge them twice a daie. Then boile them in faire water till they be tender. But you must shifte the water in your seethinge twise or thrise. Then take of your orenges and laye them on a faire clothe to coole. Then take rosewater half a pint or somwhat more to a pound of orenge and a pound of suger at the least. You must not put in all your suger at once but some and some in the seethinge amongest your orenges. Boyle them with a softe fire and when you Thincke your sirupe is somwhat thicke put in Your orenges being cold first and with them a Pippin or two and let them boile till they be So tender as you would have them. Then Take them upp and laie them one by one in a faire platter till they be colde and clarifie your sirupe with the whites of ij or iij egges beaten together. Then take of your sirrupe and when it is colde put them together.

TO MAKE CONSERVE
OF CHERYES AND
OTHER FRUITES

Take a pounde of cheryes, boile them drie
with their owne licor, then straine them
through an heavie sive. When you have strained
the cheryes put in ij pounde of fine beaten suger
and boile them together a good pretye while.
Then put your conserve in a potte.

TO MAKE CONSERVES OF ORENGES

*T*ake orenges and pare them verie thinne the red outsyde away. Then quarter them in 4 partes and take awaye the white of the insyde. Then seethe them in faire water softlye for breakinge ofte changinge them in warme water till they be boiled softe and the yelownes sodde [alternative strong aorist form of 'seethed'] awaye. As the yelownes seetheth awaie so dothe the bitternes. Then take them out of water and laye them in a faire vessell that the water maye rune

out of them. Then beate them small with a spoone
and put to everye pounde of orenges a pounde of
suger and an half pinte of good rosewater and so
boile them well together and boxe it.

TO MAKE
MARMALADE

Take quinces and pare them and cut of the cores: then seeth them verie tender in cleane water and straine them in canvas of viij *d* an ell and let them stande in the vessell wherin they be strained. Then take of the water that it is sodden in and take two whites of egges and beate it fine and put it in the same water. Then take suger and put therunto, then let seethe the same white of egges suger and the same water till it be boiled half awaye. Then take blancket lininge and straine it through the same. Then put the sirupe and quinces together. So boile them till it be verie thicke and stirre it well for burninge. Then boxe it.

A PROPORTION
TO MAKE YOUR
DISHES OF GELLYE

Take one gallon of water one gallon of good claret wine vj calfes feete and one capon. Seethe all these together softlie iiij or v howers and in the seethinge skime it cleane. Then take upp a litle of the brothe and if it will stande take upp the rest and straine it. Then to that liquor put your turnsall and the vinegar ordered as shall followe and softlie seethe your liquor againe.

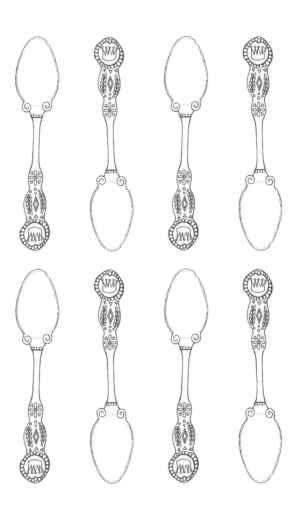

Then take upp of it and see how you like the colour and therin use your discretion. This being coloured take the whites of xiiij egges well beaten and put them into your liquor and againe therwith softlye boile your liquor ever stirringe it in the boilinge. Boilinge it but a litle while then straine it. This done put in your spices and suger.

Ye must steepe all night 1oz of turnsall in Half a pinte of good vineger and put the vinegar And the turnsall in your liquor.

Suger 1 pound and a half
Ginger 1oz
Sinamon 1oz and a half quarter
Graines half quarter oz
Longe pepper ½oz

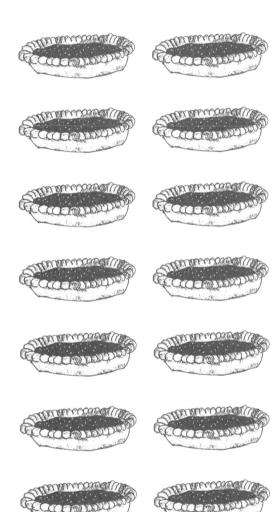

TO MAKE A TARTE

❧

Take Mellylot, Bugle, hockhele, Valarian
of eche like muche with ij croppes of
Sage stampt all these together and straine it waxe
Turpentine and a litle rosen and iiij spoonefulles
of oyle olive and boile them together; then mingle
your juise aforesaid and it together.

TO MAKE GELLYES

Take a Capon and iiij Calves feete: take your
Capon and cut him in sunder in the half
and laye him in water all night and then take out all
the skinnes and fatte in the side of the backe and
take the Calves feete and cut them in half and cut
out all the blacke and the fatte in the side Therof:
then take the capon and the feete withall and drie
them faire with a cleane clothe: then put them into
the potte that you boile in and put therto iij quartes
of white wine and a pottell of faire water and set
them over the fire of coles and let them boyle there

untill the skinne or fatte doe rise. Skimme the fatte cleane of and there let it boile untill you see parte of the gellye coole in a sawcer and then take it of and let it runne through a cleane clothe into a deape bason and let it stande and coole untill the gellie doe stande and then skimme of all the fatte that is uppermost; then take all the rest until you come to the bottome and put it into a faire earthen potte and set it over a softe fire of coles. And then take iiij nutmegges and scrape them and quarter them and take ij greate stickes of Sinamonde and scrape them cleane and cut them in peces of an inche longe: take therto half a pounde of suger and more and put it into the potte with the spice and there let it be untill the spice be sunke downe to the bottome. And then put in a spoonefull of white vineger and a litle white salt to the taste of your mouthe: and then take half a dossen of whites of egges and beate them small and a fewe fethers and put them into the potte and let them sethe a wame and then take them of and put them through a gellye bagge ix or x times. Then put it into your vessell wherin you will kepe it.

TO PRESERVE
ORENGES IN SIRUPE

Let the sirupe wherin you boile your orenges be boiled to the full heighte of a sirupe and then put in your orenges and let them boile a iust hower in the same sirupe and make the sirupe and the orenges both colde and kepe them therin. To make the sirupe Take a quantitie of verie fine flower and the yelkes and whites of egges and good thicke creame and a good deale of fine suger and if ye will a litle Sinamon and worke all these together in paste and when your

paste is readie wroughte worke amonge it some
Anis seedes and fenell seedes and then make it
upp in ringes and knottes and set on a panne of
water on the fire and make it seethe: and when
it beginneth to seethe put in these orenges and
knottes into the water and at the first puttinge in
they will fall downe to the bottome and as soone
as they rise againe take them out and laie them
uppon some table to drye and then they be drye
then bake them.

BLANC MANGER FOR ONE THAT IS SICKE

ake almondes and beate them verie fine and beate withal rosewater and verie fine suger and straine it thorough a fine clothe. Let your stuffe be as thicke as the stuffe that you make your creame tarte withall and then put ij spoonefulles of vergis to it.

ANOTHER FOR
THE SAME

*F*irst blanche almondes fine beaten vjoz and straine them with rosewater and thicken your brothe with iij or iiij whites of egges with a litle grated breade: boile them on a softe fire and then straine and season it with rosewater and suger: and so dishe it.

TO MAKE A TARTE
OF ORENGES

*T*ake orenges and shave them: then laye
them in water a nighte then perboile
them in waters. That done laye them in
Malmeseye ij howers. Then take them out from
the Malmeseye and Seethe them on the fire and
put to them ij yelkes of egges, Sinamon, suger
and a litle rosewater.

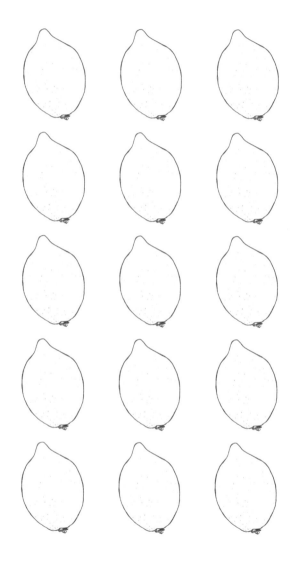

SIRUPE OF RINDES OF ORENGES OR LEMONS

*T*ake rindes while they be newe and freshe one pounde good fine runninge water v wine pintes: sethe them unto iij pintes. Then straine it and with one pounde of suger seethe it to the height of a sirupe and when it is taken from the fire put into the sirupe iiij grains of muske if you will have it good. This sirupe strenghteneth the stomacke the braine and the harte. If the disease come of colde it maketh a swete breathe. The rindes of orenges or lemons made in

conserve doe the like. The rindes of orenges
be verie bitter and for that cause they be laid in
socke a space to take the bitternes awaye before
they be made in conserve.

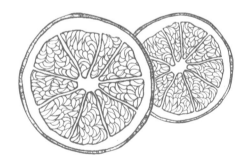

TO PRESERVE
DAMSONS

ake a pound of damsons with the stalkes on them and half a pounde of good white suger beaten verie fine and xij spoonefulles of red rosewater, xiij whole cloves unbeaten, viij peces of Sinamon of an inche longe put all these in an earthen potte or panne and set the stalkes of the damsons upwarde and set them over a softe fire of imbers till the sirupe be thicke then it will hange uppon a spoone: then take it of the fire xij howers: then take them out of the panne and

put them in a glasse and stoppe them close that
no ayer come to them and so you maie kepe
them a yere if you will. Within half a yere if
you thincke the damsons beginne to venewe
take awaye the venewinge of them and seethe
the sirupe againe with a quantitie of suger and
rosewater which suger must be beaten verie
fine or it be put into the rosewater.

TO PRESERVE QUINCES ALL THE YERE

Cut out the cores of your quinces and save them, set faire water on the fire and put the cores into it and quinces with them while the water is colde and take them from the fire before they sethe and let them soke in the water till they be softe but let them not breake. Then take them upp and laye them on a table with the holes downewarde and let them lye xij howers to coole.

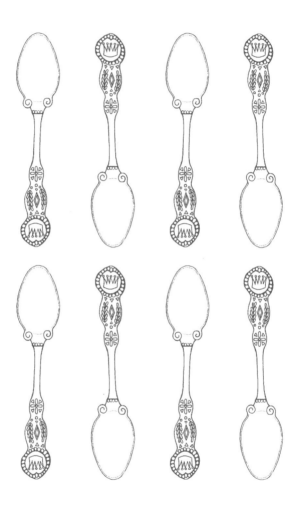

Then put them into an earthen potte and straine
the same liquor that they were sodden in and put it
into the potte and close it from the ayre and when
you take anye out save the rine whole as neare as
you can. Take xxx quinces and make not the holes
to bigge and laye them in faire water. Then take for
everye iij quinces a pounde of suger of the finest ye
can gette and for everye x quinces a gallon of water
and set it on a softe fire of coles that it smoke not
and put in the suger after the quinces aforesaide
and take a couple of the whites of egges and beate
them in a dishe with a spoone and put them into
the same water and suger and with a sticke all cut
and iagged stirre the same sirupe a good while and
make it to seethe softlie and then skimme of the
skumme that you shall see uppon the sirupe verie
cleane so that you leave nothing uppon it and when
it will cast no more skimme then take it of the
fire, then straine it thorow half a yarde of wollen
clothe sacke as you runne Ipocras thorough into
another panne of faire water and boile them faire
and softly a litle so that in no wise ye breake them:
and when they be indifferentlie well sodden then
take them out and laye them on a faire bourde
with the cores downe warde that the water maye

runne of and out of them. Take your sirupe and set it on the fire againe and make it boile againe. In the meane season take the quinces and pricke in everie of them ij or iij cloves and let them boile and in anye wise tourne them with a pretye sticke that they be no more boiled on the one side then on the other: and in anye wise see they breake not and skimme of such skimme as you shall see arise of them: and then put into xxx quinces half a pint of red rosewater and put in whole stickes of Sinamon of an handful longe a pece and breake them into small peces of an inche longe and put them into the sirupe with the quinces and let them boile a while, after you have put in the sirupe: then take them out and put them into a faire charger and laye the wholes downewarde that they maie all drie cleane and let the sirupe seethe and stande still uppon the fire and let it coole. Then put the quinces into a newe earthen potte and powre the sirupe to them and cover it close with a paper over the pottes mouthe and a faire clothe over the paper fast bounde about the pottes mouthe and let them stande a monethe.

TO MAKE QUINCES
IN SIRUPE

*T*ake xxx quinces to the quantitie of this
sirupe take a pottell of water and put it
in a panne and then take the whites of vj egges
and beate them with another pottell of water and
then put it all together and put therwith xij or xiiij
pounds of suger as you see cause and seethe it
and skomme it cleane and then put therto ijoz of
cloves and bruse them a verie litle and let them
sethe till the skomme arise verie blacke and then
skomme of the cloves againe and washe them

in faire water and drie them and put them in
againe and your quinces also and let them sethe a
quarter of an hower and not past and put to them
half a pinte of rosewater: and then put this sirupe
in a faire earthen panne and laye a sheete iiij
double upon it to kepe it in the heate and then
let it stande a daye or two: and then put them and
the sirupe in a vessell that was never occupied
and cover them close. But in the beginninge pare
your quinces and core them and then seethe
them in faire water till they be verie tender and
then take them upp and laye them that the water
maye runne from them cleane. And when they
be almost colde then put them in your sirupe as
is above said.

TO MAKE CONSERVE
OF BARBERIES

*T*ake your Barberies and picke them cleane and set them over a softe fire and put the rose water as muche as ye thincke meete. Then when ye thincke it be sodden inough straine that and then sethe it againe and to everye pounde of pulpe take one pounde of suger and make your conserve.

TO MAKE GELLYE

First ye must take iiij calves feete and a knockle of veale take out the fatte and the greate bones and leave none but the sinewes and the ioyntes: and likewise of the calves feete take out the bones. This done take a potte of suche quantitie as ye shall mete and fill it full of water and put your meate in and let it sethe half awaye then fill it upp with wine: and let it seethe till it will gellye in a spoone. Then take it of and straine it from the meate and let it stande till it be colde: Then take of the uppermost and the clearest: and then set it over the fire and put in spices and suger and viij whites of egges beaten with an handfull of fethers and also a spoonefull of vineger. Then put in all togethers and let them sethe ij or iij walmes over the fire: and in the meane time put into the bagge iij or iiij branches of rosemarie and ij of Margerom. Then let your gellye runne thorough the bagge till it be cleare.

TO MAKE A BLANCHMAME ON THE FISHE DAYE

Take the whites of egges and Creame and boile them on a chafinge dishe of Coles till they curde: then will there a whaye goe from them: put awaye the whaye and put to the Curde a litle rosewater: then straine it and season it with suger.

TO MAKE RICE
POREGE

Take rise and washe it Cleane and laye it in water all night and in the morninge power the water from it and put it in a platter and set it before the fire and let it drye till it be readie to breake. Then put it in a Bladder to kepe for what use you will and when you make Porege let the milke sethe first and put therto as muche Rice as you thincke will make it thicke with pepper salt Cloves and mace and suger and so let it sethe till the rice be tender and so serve it.

TO MAKE THICKE CREAME WITH RICE

Take dryed ryce and beate it fine and straine it with the Creame and let it boile on a platter on a chafinge dishe of coles till it be verie thicke: then season it with a litle rosewater and suger and when you thincke it is thicke inough take it of and when it is colde serve it forthe with ij rewes on a dishe.

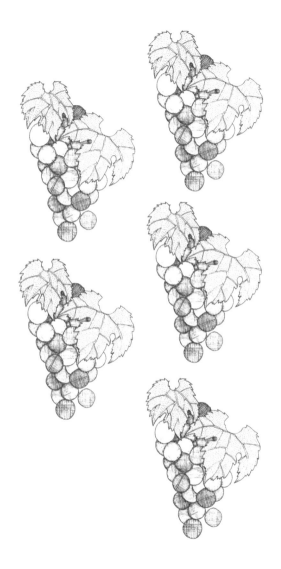

TO MAKE SIRUPE
OF GRAPES

*T*ake your grapes and stampe them and see ye beate not the kernelles of them but if you Cannot chose: and then straine them and put that licor that cometh of them and a good plentye of suger. Let it sethe longe till it will abide uppon your naile and then it is well and so take it upp and kepe it: it is verie good to kepe one moiste. See you kepe it close.

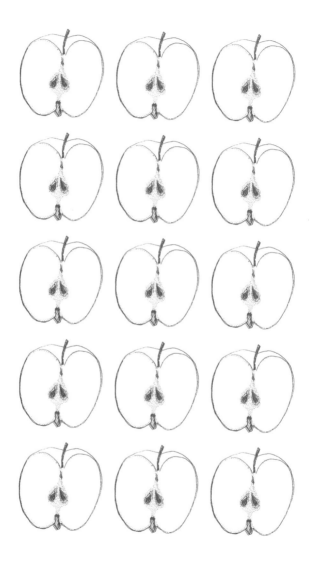

TO MAKE A TARTE
OF PRUNES

*F*irst sethe your prunes in water and wine
and for lacke of wine take a litle ale and
a good handfull of slyced apples amongest them
with iij or iiij slyces of a manchet and when they
be tender straine them and season them with
Sinamon ginger rosewater and suger.

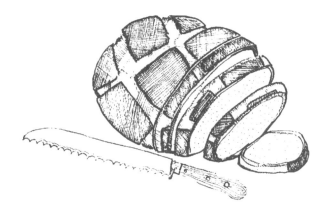

TO MAKE A TARTE
OF WARDENS

*T*ake wardens and put them in a potte and cover the potte with dowe and let them bake with householde breade and when they be colde season them with suger Sinamon ginger rosewater and a litle nutmegge.

TO MAKE A CLEARE
TARTE OF DAMSONES

Take damsones when they be full ripe
and put them in a potte and stoppe the
potte with dowe and bake them till they be verye
tender: then uncover the potte and power out
the damsones into a strainer and let the sirupe
runne from them without anye pressinge and
take the sirupe and put it in an earthen potte and
let it boile with as muche suger as will make it
pleasaunt till it be as stiffe as gellye. Then make
your Tarte and set it in the oven and when it is

through hardened powre in the sirupe and let it bake: and if it be not stiffe inoughe ye maye let it stande the longer in the oven and serve it colde without anye thinge uppon it. Let it be no stiffer then gellie.

TO MAKE A TARTE
OF BARBERIES

Take Eglentline berries when they be almost ripe and picke all that is within them and washe them cleane and put them in an earthen potte with halfe wine halfe water and let them boile till they be softe: Then strue them and season them with suger Sinamon ginger and a litle rosewater and a litle butter.

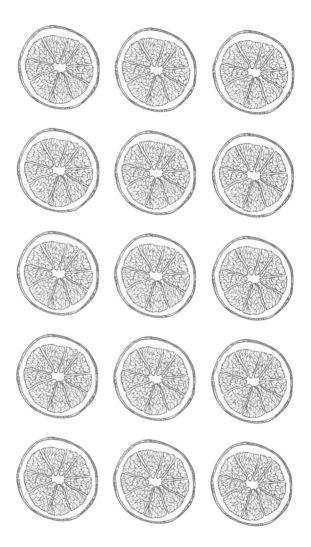

TO MAKE A TARTE
OF ORENGES

*T*ake orenges and pare them as thinne as you can then cut them in the middest and with your thumbe take out all the meate and laye the skinne in water ij nightes and a daye and change the water divers times. Then sethe them in iiij or v waters till they be tender and laye them in Malmseye 4 or 5 howers and wringe them out and straine them with Malmseye and a litle rosewater and ij or iij yolkes of egges and set it on a chafinge dishe of coles and let it harden a litle and season it with suger Sinamon and ginger.

A TARTE AFTER THE FRENCH FASHION

✣

*T*ake a pinte of creame and the yolkes of x egges and beate them together and put therto as much suger as will make it swete and half a dishe full of butter and boile these together till they be thicke and make one Couple of Cakes and laye your meate when it is colde in one of them and cover it with the other and cut the Cover long wise and bake it with an yse of rosewater and suger uppon it.

TO PRESERVE
DAMSONES

Take your damsones the stalkes beinge of them and Washe them and take to vj pounde of damsones, iiij Pounde of suger with xij spoonefulles of rosewater and set your panne over the fire with the rosewater in it: then put in some of your suger and when it is melted put in some Sinamon stickes with xij Cloves brused and with all your Damsones and the rest of your suger. Then cover your panne close and so let them stewe verie softlie the space of ij howers and some times stirre them with a spoone for burninge to. And when you see your sirupe verie thicke put them in your glasse.

TO PRESERVE
DAMSONES

Take a pinte of rosewater and set it over the fire and put therto iij pounde of suger with Sinamon stickes and Cloves brused and let these sethe till the sirupe be verie thicke. Then put in some of your damsones and let them sethe as softlie as is possible and when they be tender take them out and set your sirupe on the fire againe and put then in no damsones. And when they be tender take them out and so use as manye as you thincke your sirupe will kepe. Then let your sirupe sethe with a litle more suger till it be verie thicke because the damsones make it thinner with lyinge in it.

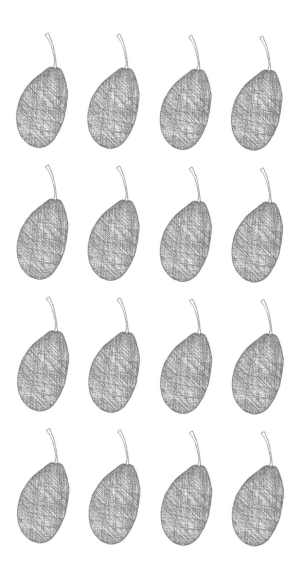

TO MAKE GELLYE

First take the knockell of veale and cut the ioyntes all to peces and laye them in faire water the space of an hower: then washe them and laye them in faire water the space of half an hower: then take a faire potte and put your fleshe in it and fill your potte with claret wine and water and set it on the fire and skimme it as cleane as you can and let it boile verie softlye. For the sooner it is boyled the longer it wilbe or it come to a gellye. And when it is boiled then straine the liquor into a faire bole and when it is colde take a

spoone and take of the fatte and then take out the
clearest and put in a faire potte and sethe it: Then
put in your suger, Sinamon ginger, graines, cloves
longe pepper, nutmegges take of eche of these
like quantitie and bruse them: then serce out the
small peces and put the greatest into your potte
and when it boileth put in the whites of egges
and butter. Then take a skommer and skomme
them as they rise. Then drie your turnesole by
the fire and rubbe it cleane and color your gellye
therwith. Then take your bagg and rosemarye in
the bottome of it and hange it by the fire syde and
let your gellye runne ij times thorough your bagge
into a faire vessell.

A WAYE TO MAKE
HYPOCRAS

*ake a gallon of wine and an ounce of Sinamon, ij ounces of ginger, a pounde of suger, xx cloves brused and xx cromes of pepper bigge beaten and so let all these soke together all one nighte and let it runne through a bagge and it wil be good.

TO MAKE A
GOOD GELLYE

Take iiij Calves feete and skalde the
heare of them and then sethe them
in faire water till they be tender: then take out
your feete and let the brothe runne through a
Colender and so let your brothe stande till it
be Colde and then ye shall take the fatte cleane
from it. And then put Claret wine and a litle
Malmsey to your gellye: and if you have a pottell
of gellie water then put to it one quarte of wine

and a pinte of Malmsey: Then season it with salt and put therto a pounde of suger an ounce and an half of Sinamon and an ounce of ginger xx Cornes of pepper xx cloves and a litle Saffron and so boile all together. Then take a good sawcer full of vineger and turnesole into your gellye. And when it is well sodden that the strenght of the spice be felt then take out your turnesole and set by the gellie till it be somwhat Cooled and then put in your beaten whites of egges and let all have a boyle together. Then set all by and in a while let it runne through your bagge.

TO MAKE CONSERVE
OF ROSES

*T*ake to everye ounce of rose leave iijoz of suger and cut awaye the white from them and beate them in a stone morter untill they be so small as is possible. When you have so done put therto the foresaid quantitie of suger: and whatsoever flowers you will make conserve of you must take to everie ounce of flowers iijoz of suger.

TO MAKE OYLE
OF ROSES

First you must take red roses and bruse them a litle: then take to everie ounce of roseleave vjoz of oyle olive and put to it: stoppe it verye fast and close: Then let your glasse stande in the whotest place of the sunne that you can finde xv dayes: Then take it and warme it, then straine it and wringe it through a clothe so harde as you maye: and this is good of roses. But if you will have it verie fine then let it stande no longer but x or xij dayes and then straine it: and when you

have strained the oyle from the rose leaves then
put freshe leaves to the same oyle and let them
stande so longe in it or longer then thother did
and then straine it and wringe it out harde and
this will be good.

TO MAKE SIRUPE OF
DAMASKE ROSES

*F*irst you must take red roses and picke them cleane and the white cut awaye: then take runninge water and set it over the fire till it be readye to seethe: then take it from the fire and put it in an earthen vessell and to everye gallon of water a pounde of roses: So let them xij howers and then straine them with a linnen clothe: and then set the liquor over the fire againe till it be readie to sethe. Then put it in the earthen vessell againe with newe roses and so must you doe iij or v dayes together changinge the roses everie xii howers as you did before kepinge the mouth of the vessell verie close and at the end of five dayes you maye clense the liquir from the roses and set it over the fire and to a gallon of liquor you must put a pounde of suger or more sethinge it till it be like a sirupe. If you take ij gallons of water in the beginninge it wilbe scarcelye at the dayes and you must wringe the roses verie harde through the Clothe at everie change.

TO PRESERVE
DAMSONES

*F*irst take your damsones beinge never to ripe for burstinge neyther to greene for putrifyinge: washe them cleane and drye them with a linnen clothe: then take an earthen potte cover the bottome with fine suger and laye your damsones in the same so that they touche not one another: then set your potte over a Charcole fire let them boile till they doe once cracke: then take of your potte and put therin whole Sinamon whole Cloves and a litle muske tyed in a linen clothe:

then let it stande it Covered till it be so well soked
that the meate will come cleane from the stone
with ease. Then take upp your damsones and laye
them in a faire platter strowe suger uppon them
and so to stande till they be through colde. Then
take your sirupe and sethe it with suger till it be
verie thicke and when it is through colde put your
sirupe and damsones with the foresaid spices into
a glasse and so you maye preserve them as longe
as you will renewinge them on the fire with suger
once a quarter.

TO MAKE PRUNES IN SIRUPE

*T*ake your prunes and put claret wine to them and suger as ye thincke will make them swete and pleasaunt and so let all seethe together till ye thincke the liquor looke like a sirupe and that the prunes be well swollen and so kepe them in a vessell as ye doe greene ginger.

TO PRESERVE
ORENGES

Take your orenges and pare the uttermost
rinde of and then scotche the rinde as ye
doe apples to roste with shorte scotches and then
laye them in water: chaunge them thrise a daye
and so doe ij or iij dayes: then thrushe out your
kernelles in the scotches: and then sethe your
orenges in cleane water: ever amonge them the
water hath changed Colder put a newe sethinge
water to them and put out the olde. Then when

you thincke the bitternes is well gone that the
water looke not yelowe and that your orenges be
tender then take them out and laye them a drying
and then take a pottell of water xx orenges and
iij pounds of suger and let your orenges and all
boile together till they be to a sirupe that it will
stande somwhat stiffe and ass the skumme riseth
take it of and then so kepe them: and if ye will
bake them ye maye put if ye will of that sirrupe to
them or none if ye will. And this is good.

TO MAKE GOOD ORENGEARD

*T*ake half an hundreth of orenges and cut them in iij or iiij partes and take awaye the core of the orenges and then laye them in faire water the outter side of the orenge iiij or v dayes and that change thrise a daye: and then set them over the fire in cleane water and let them sethe till they be as tender as ye thincke by reason metelye: and then laye them on a dire borde ij or iij dayes that the water maye Consume and then take viij pounde of suger powder or els of lofe suger whether ye will: clarifye it with white of egges. Take vij egges and then take the white of them and a litle cleane water and with a spoone breake the whites of the egges and the water together: then take ij or iij gallons of faire water and put your whites of egges unto the same water and the viij pounde of suger and let it sethe and as the skomme risethe let it be skimmed. For the egges will suffer no evill thinge in it and let the water and the suger sethe together from ij or iij gallons to a pottell or more and then straine it through a blanket such as men have in their hosen and let the blancket be cleane washed and wringe out the water and even white as it is let the sirupe rinne thorough: and then set it on the fire againe and let it boyle till the water be consumed awaye: then put in your orenges and let them boile softlye till the sirupre waxe somewhat stiffe. Then take it from the fire and let it coole and ye shall have good orengeard and everye daye better. For when the fire is out it wilbe verie pleasaunt.

TO STEWE QUINCES

First pike out the core cleane and then fill the hole full with small reasones and then put them in an earthen thinne potte and let your proportion be after the forme followinge, that is to saye, if your potte be of the quantitie of a pottell then take a quarte of well water and red wine and put therto a pounde of suger and this waye shall suffice, put therto a quantitie of ginger and a quantitie of Sinamond. And when you have this done put your sirupe into your potte and put your potte into the imbers and then let them soke till they be tender.

HOW TO PRESERVE
FRUITES

*T*ake ij pounds of quinces and cut them in small peces: then take a quarte of faire water and sethe it till it come to a pinte and then let it runne through a faire clothe and then put in half a pounde of suger and let it boile not faste: then pare a quince and core it and put it to it and allwayes be tourninge of it and let the Codiniake boile till it stande on your nayle like a perle and then it will be red. You must take as muche suger as gooseberies to a pounde of gooseberies and

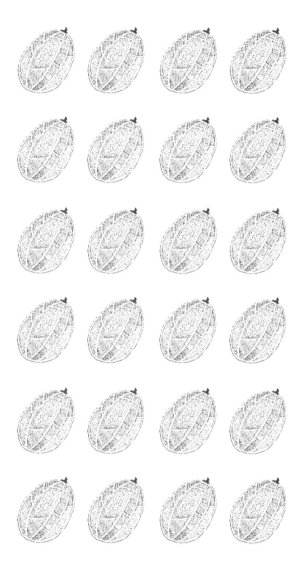

3 quarters of a pinte of rosewater and put them all together and set them on the fire and let them simper verie softlie while the sirupe looketh red.

If you enjoyed this book, you may also be interested in…

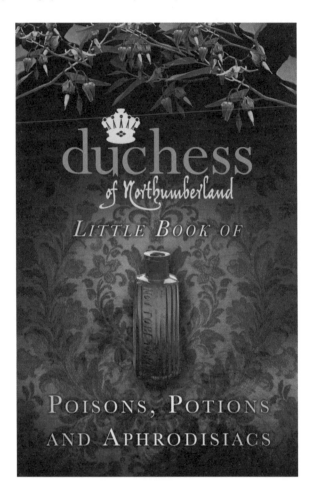